MW00946035

SHIVA SWARODAYA

A Divine Law Of Breathing

MOHAN KUMAR

"Vakratunda Mahakaya Suryakoti
Samaprabha Nirvighnam Kuru Me
Dev Sarva Karyesu Sarvada"

PREFACE

Lord Shiva is the God of Gods. He is the creator, observer and destroyer of the world. All the sciences and technologies are given by him. Maheshwara (shiva) gave all these knowledge to her wife Goddess Parvati (devi Parvati) at first. Later, on Parvati's prayer, he gave this knowledge and sciences to Sapt Maharishis and Devi Parvati (devine or sacred seven saints) for the welfare of the human beings. Among all the ancient sciences, 'Shiv Swarodaya' is one of the best science, which is very useful for all the people of the world. It is a book of the process and law of 'Breathing' or 'Respiration'. All lilving things on earth breath air without which we can't survive on earth.

Animals, trees, birds and human beings everyone breathe to survive. But there is a lot of way of breathing. Breathing is not just to pump our blood but it is the life. Life is possible on earth and is fully depends on breathing. But if we know the process and law of breathing then we can survive thousands of years on earth. Our ancestors live more than one hundred years. Ancient saints and Maharishis (great saints) could survive thousands of years and even in modern times there are many Great Saints, who meditate or penance from thousands of years in the Himalayan caves. They can survive till now, even without eating food, only by the law or process of respiration.

Shiv Swarodaya is the book of 'law or process of Respiration or

Breathing'. On Parvati's prayer, God Shiva gave this knowledge of science to her for the welfare of human beings. This book describes the conversation between them and also describes the science.

Shiv Swarodaya book is very useful for all types of person on earth. You can get many benefits by following this book. It can change your life. If you are ill then you can be healthy. If you are weak by this book you can become powerful. You can make your body as tough (or strong) as iron. You can also survive many days, weeks or years without food by practicing this. You can survive more than hundred years. This book also help you to get supernatural powers, if you are a Yogi (or Sadhak). You can survive many hours, even days or years under water

3

by the law of breathing. You can also survive on coldest and hottest region where no one can survive.

The book 'Shiv Swarodaya' is a devine and sacred book. It is the collection of ancient sciences of India. Ancient scientist of India is also known as 'Maharishi' or 'Rishi'. They practiced the law or process of Swara (breathing) and become super humans. Even in modern times many Sadhus or Yogis (saints) are present who is very powerful and have supernatural powers. 'Karodimal Baba' is one of the example who survive many years and worshipped as God by many people of the world. Mark Zuckerberg and many more person also meet with him and get blessings from him and become successful. He also follow the law of breathing (swara) or "Shiv Swarodaya". If you follow this book then definitely you will become a successful person and even a super human.

MOHAN KUMAR

(MOHAN MURARI)

SHIVASVARODAYA

With salutations to Mahesvara (Shiva), Sailaja (Parvati), Gananayak (Ganesh), and Guru (Perceptor), I remember the Supreme Lord who redeems all from the bondage of the world.

Devi said :

O God of Gods ! O Lord ! Take mercy on me and reveal to me the knowledge which bestows all prosperity and benefits.

6

O God ! How did this Universe originate, how it changes and how dissolves – tell me that which is the determiner of the Universe.

Ishwara said :

O Goddess ! This Universe originates from the Elements; the Elements preserve it, and in the Elements it finally dissolves. Thus, understand it as determined by the Elements.

Devi said :

Certainly the philosophers have decided the Elements as the final substance of the Universe, but kindly

7

reveal to me the nature of the
Elements.

Ishwara said :

There is one Supreme Lord
devoid of Maya and Form; from Him
originated the Akasa (sky) and from
Akasha the Vayu (wind).

From Vayu originated Teja (Fire),
from Teja the Waters and from waters
the Earth. These are the five elements
and each of these is further
differentiated into five – thus in all
there come into existence twenty-five
Elements.

8

My Beauty ! In the body, which originates from the Five elements, reside all these Five Elements in subtle form. All the Tatva – Yogis know this.

Now I describe the science of the origin of the Swaras which reside in the body. With the knowledge of he Swaras, which move in the form of 'Hamsah', one acquires the knowledge of the past, present and future.

This science of Swara is a secret of all secrets and reveals the secret of the essence of all benefits. This science is the crest jewel of all knowledge.

This subtle of the subtlest of knowledge is worth through mastery. It appears a wonder to the non –

9

believers and is the foundation for those who are believers.

Characteristics of Shisya

This science of Swarodaya should be taught to a disciple (Sisya) whose nature is composed and pure, who is of good character and has firm faith in his Guru, is obedient, and is obliged to the acts of kindness done to him.

This science should not be impated to one who is wicked, non believer, intemperate, of lose character, of an irritable nature and commits adultery on his Guru's wife.

O Devi ! Listen now to what I tell about that knowledge which resides in the body and by the mere knowledge of which one becomes omniscient.

All the Vedas, Shastras, Music, and all the three worlds are inherent in the Swaras and the Swaras are identical with Atman.

An astrologer without a knowledge of the Swara, a house without an owner, a mouth without Shastras, and a body without a head are never acclaimed.

A person who knows the three fold differentiation of Nadis in the form of Nadis, Prana – Tattva and Susumna, attains emancipation.

11

The manifest (practical) and the formless (spiritual) become auspicious only on the strength of the Wind (Swara); and O Varanane (of beautiful face, i.e. Parvati) ! some say that the knowledge of Swara at once gives auspicious results.

The part and whole of the Universe are made up of Swara. The Generator and Destroyer of the Universe is really the Swara in the form of Maheswara.

No one has ever seen or heard of a quality beyond the knowledge of Swaras, any wealth beyond the knowledge of Swaras, and any knowledge beyond the knowledge of Swaras.

12

If one has the strength of Swara only then he should attack his foe or meet his friend. Wealth (Lakshmi), fame and pleasure and comfort are all obtained through the strength of Swaras.

Travel becomes possible by the strength of Swaras; food is obtained by the strength of Swaras; and even urination and defecation are made possible by the strength of Swaras.

Marriage of daughter, audience from a king, kindness of a God or the subjugation of a king become possible only by virtue of Swaras.

O Lady of beautiful face ! all the Shaastras, Puranas, Smritis and the Vedangas are nothing beyond the knowledge of Swaras

As long as there is no knowledge of the Elements the illusion of name and form remains a futility and so long the ignorants also remain baffled.

The science of Swarodaya (knowledge of the rise of breathing in one or the other nostril) is higher than the highest of the Shastras, and is like the wick of the lamp to illumine the pot in the form of Atman.

The science of Swarodaya should not be imparted to all and sundry who happen to ask for it, but it should be

14

mastered for one's own self by one's own intellect in his own body.

There is no obstruction of Tithi (days of the lunar fort night), asterisms, week days, planets, Deity, Bhadra (name of the second, seventh and twelfth day of a lunar fortnight), Vyatipata (a portent foreboding a great calamity), or unsteadiness of conditions (i.e. this science can be practised at any time and in any condition).

Neither there ever had been nor there ever would be an inauspicious moment for it. When the pure strength of the Swaras is available all results are auspicious.

15

There are numerous Nadis of different sizes in the body and they shluld be known by the erudites for the knowledge about their own bodies.

Originating like sprouts from the root situated a little above the navel, there are 72000 Nadis in the body.

In the Nadis, sleeps the Serpent-like structure Kundalini Shakti. Ten Nadis go upwards from the root-point and ten also downwards in the body. Two Nadis each go in oblique directions which thus make twentyfour in all. Out of these ten are the main Nadis which provide the flow of Wind in the body.

All the Nadis of the body, going oblique, upwards or downwards, are situated in the form of a Chakra and are under the sway of Prana (vayu).

Out of ten, which have been said to be the main Nadis, there are only three, viz. the *Ida, Pingla, and Susumna*, which should be regarded as most important.

The names of remaining seven (apart from *Ida, Pingal, and Susumna)* are *Gandhari, Hastajihva, Pusa, Yasasvini, Alambusa, Kuhu, and Sankhini.*

Ida is situated on the left (side of the spinal cord), Pingala on the right and Susumna in the middle (of the Spinal cord). Gandhari is situated in the left and Hastajihva in the right

17

eye; Pusa in the right ear, Yasasvini in the left ear; Alambusa in the mouth; Kuhu in the genital organ, and the Sankhini in the anus. In this manner are the ten Nadis situated in the ten gates of the body.

All these ten Nadis are situated in the middle of the body and the Ida, Pingala and the Susumna are situated in the passage of the Prana.

I now enumerate the names of the winds which flow through the Nadis. These are Prana, Apana, Samana, Udana, and Vyana; Naga, Kurma, Krkala, Devadatta and Dhananjaya. The Prana-vayu resides in the heart and the Apana-vayu in the anus.

Samana is sutuated in the naval region, Udana at the centre of the neck, and the Vyana flows all over the body. These ten Vayus or winds are most important.

There are five Prana etc, and five Naga etc, sets of Vayus (winds). The places of the first five have already been described. I now describe the places of the remaining five Naga etc., Vayus.

In vomitting one should know the Naga Vayu to be inherent and in the winking of eyes the Kurma Vayu. The Krkala is inherent in sneezing and the Devadatta in yawning.

The Dhananjaya Vayu, which pervades the entire body, does not leave the body even after death. In this manner the ten Vayus roam in the body.

The erudites should know that the vital winds flowing in the centre of the body are controlled by the Ida, Pingala and Susumna.

Ida should be known as situated on the left side of the spinal cord and Pingala on the right side in the reverse form.

The moon resides in the Ida, the Sun in the Pingala and the Hamsa in the Susumna – this Hamsa is Sambhu

(Shiva). Thus Hamsa in the form of Sambhu resides in the Susumna.

The process of exahalation is said to contain the alphabet *Ha* and the inhalation contains the alphabet *Sa*. *Ha-kara* (the alphabet Ha) is the form of *Shiva* and the *Sa-kara* (the alphabet Sa) the form of *Shakti*.

The controller of the flow of the left Nadi (i.e. Ida, which flows through the left nostril) is Moon who also resides in it in the form of Shakti. The controller of the flow of the right Nadi (i.e. Pingala, which flows through the right nostril) is the Sun who also resides in it in the form of Sambhu (Shiva).

21

A Yogi of concentrated and composed mind should see only through this path and regard everything contained only in the path of the Moon and the Sun, (i.e. the paths of the flow of the wind through Ida and Pingala respectively).

One should concentrate upon the Elements only when his mind is composed and undisturbed. Thus he archieves the desired results, benefits and victory. One should not concentrate upon them in a disturbed state of mind.

Mastery over the knowledge of past and present comes to one who practices thoroughly the Moon and the Sun Swaras.

The left Nadi Ida is Nectar-like (Amrta-swarup) and supports the entire world. The right Nadi Pingala always creates the entire world.

The Nadi in the middle (i.e. Susumna) is cruel and inauspicious for all occasions; while the left Nadi is always auspicious and bestows fructification of all actions.

The left Nadi is auspicious at the time of proceeding for a work while the right is auspicious on the return. Therefore, one should always consider the Moon as even and virtuous and the Sun as uneven and non-virtuous.

The Moon is a female. The Sun is a Male. The complexion of the Moon is fair and that of the Sun dark. When the Moon Nadi (ida) is flowing then good and amiable works should be undertaken.

When the Sun Nadi (Pingala or the right nostril) is flowing then cruel and daring works should be undertaken. When Susumna is flowing then amorous, sexual and such acts which lead to emancipation, should be undertaken.

On the first day of the dark fortnight the Sun Swara (i.e. right nostril) flows, and the Moon Swara (i.e. left nostril) flows on the first day of the lighted fortnight. These Swaras remain powerful on the first three days of their respective fortnights.

Beginning with the Moon Swara in the lighted fortnight these Swaras alternate during 24 hours of the day and night at the rate of 5/2 Ghatis each, i.e. each Swara alternates 24 times in one day and night.

And in each of these 5/2 Ghatis each of the Elements rules for half a Ghati during the reign of flow of the Sun or Moon Swara. If the Swara flow against the specification for each of the fortnights, i.e. if instead of the Moon Swara the Sun is flowing and vice-versa, then it must be regarded as inauspicious and therefore should be avoided.

The Yogis should with concentrated mind know the Moon Swara on the first day of the lighted

25

fortnight and the Sun Swara on the first day of the dark fortnight.

The Moon Swara should be avoided in the night and the Sun Swara in the day. One who practices in this manner is really a Yogi, there in no doubt about it.

The Sun is bound by the Sun Swara and the Moon by the Moon Swara. One who knows this can captivate the three worlds in a moment.

If the Sun Swara rises at the time of the Moon Swara but sets at its own time, i.e., at the time of the Sun Swara, then various group of qualities (auspicious) arise. If the condition is contrary to this it should be avoided.

On Thursday, Friday, Wednesday and Monday the left Nadi (flow of the left nostril) is auspicious for all occasions, and in the lighted fortnight it is all the more effective.

For roving business (works which require movements from one place to another) the right Nadi (i.e. flow of the right nostril) should be considered favourable on Sunday, Tuesday, and Saturday. It becomes all the more effective in the dark fortnight.

The order of the prevalence of the Elements is as follows : first of all the Vayu (wind) elements flows,

27

followed by the Agni (fire), Earth (prithvi), Water (Varuna or Jal), and Sky (Akash) respectively.

In a period of 5/2 Ghatis all the Elements rule successively in the order enumerated previously; but also during the flow of each Nadi the five elements flow in the same order.

At the middle of a day and night one should know twelve transitional points (from one zodiacal point to another) between the Sun and the Moon. During the day time the transition of the Moon occurs from Vrisa to Karka, Kanya, Vrschika, Makara, and Mina respectively.

28

The transition of the Sun should be known from Mesa to Simha, Kumbha, Tula, Mithuna and Dhanu. In this manner one should determine the auspicious and inauspicious nature from the rising and setting of the zodiacal signs.

The Moon stays in the East and North while the Sun in the South and West. When the right nostril is flowing one should avoid going to the south and west.

One should no go to the East and North during the flow of the left nostril. If he goes in these directions then there is an apprehension of fear from the enemy; and if one insists on going he would never return.

29

Therefore, sensible persons who think of the benefit of all should not go in the directions prohibited above. If they would go they may meet death.

If on the second day of the lighted fortnight there is Moon Swara at the time of the flow of the Sun then it is beneficial for the person. If he undertakes sover and pious works on such an occasion he will derive much pleasure and benefit out of it.

On any day or night when at the time of rising of the Sun there is Sun Swara and at the time of rising of the Moon there is Moon Swara then any work at that time would be successful.

When there is Sun at the time of Moon or Moon at the time of the Sun then there would be nothing except tension, conflict and loss, and nothing auspicious can happen at that time.

Intelligent person say that under the flow of the Sun one can have the knowledge of the unseen and unheard things; while under the flow of the Moon the results are reversed, i.e. no knowledge of the unseen or unheard can be obtained.

The day on which since morning there is a rise of the adverse Swara i.e. rise of the Swara other than that specified for that day and time (moon instead of the sun or vice versa), then one should know the results as follows :

31

On the first instance there is mental anxiety, on the second instance there is loss of wealth, on the third instance unwanted travelling and on the fourth instance loss of what is desired.

On the fifth instance destruction of one's kingdom, on the sixth instance loss of all benefits, on the seventh instance there is disease and pain, and on the eighth there may be the possibility of death. (by instances here is menat the order of the alternating frequencies of the Swaras during the day and night).

In the morning, at mid-day and evening if the rise of adverse Swaras as specified above continues for eight

32

days then the effect would always be inauspicious and adverse. This would proportionately reduce if there is some regularity also in the flow of the Swaras during the period.

On a day when in the morning and at mid-day the Moon Swara flows and in the evening there is the Sun Swara then on that day there will be victory and gain. If it is contrary to this then it should be avoided otherwise destructive results would follow.

When one is proceeding on a journey or is going out for some work then he should determine the Swara that is flowing at the moment and then put only the same foot forward on the first instance (i.e. left foot if the left Swara is flowing and the right foot if the right Swara is flowing). If he starts in this manner his journey would be successful.

If the Moon Swara is flowing then even number of feet (2-4-6) should be put forward and if the Sun Swara is flowing odd number of feet (1-3-5) should be put forward. If one proceeds in this manner his journey would be successful.

At the time of getting out of the bed in the morning one should touch his mouth by the palm of that hand whose side of the Swara is running at the moment. One who does so obtains, desired results.

34

While giving or accepting charity
if one does so with the same hand
whose Swara is running or if at the
time of going out of his house puts
that foot forward whose Swara is
running then he does not meet loss,
conflict or attack of the enemy. On the
other hand by doing so he remains free
of all troubles.

If one wants to get his objectives
fulfilled by his preceptor, rlatives, king
or his minister, then he should do so
by taking some fruits in his hand. Thus
his desire would get full fruits.

While litting fire, performing
unrighteous actions like theft or
righteous actions like punishing the
opponents, one should do so empty

35

handed and that will lead him to victory, comfort and success.

Some say that one should proceed on a journey to some far off place when the Moon Swara is flowing and to a near by place under the Sun Swara.

Whatever benefits etc., have been said above acrue at the time of war only if the respective Swaras are flowing in their full strength.

If the flow of Swara is zero then according to Shiva the results are adverse.

The full strength of a Swara is not favorable in such cruel actions as extirpation of the wicked in behavior, intelligent swindling of the enemy, theft and anger of one's master.

The Moon Swara is auspicious for one who is proceeding on a journey to some distant place. This provides undisturbed fulfilment of the desired results. The Sun Swara is auspicious on the return journey.

The favourable Swara makes impossible works possible while the unfavourable Swara makes possible works impossible. Therefore one should adjust his behaviour according to the Swaras.

When the Moon Swara is running one can bear crimes even of others, when Sun Swara is running even a strong person can be subjugated. When Susumna is running one can obtain emancipation. In this manner only one God (swara) has a threefold existence.

One should make efforts to run his Swara according to the auspicious or inauspicious work which he intends to perform either in the day or at night.

Effects of the flow of Moon (Ida)

The flow of the Ida(left nstril) in favourable for: Stationary work, collection of ornaments and other

38

necessities of the house, going to a distant place, construction of a hermitage, temple, pool, well and tank, consecration of the idol of a Deity, journey, charity, marriage, and for the purchase of clothings and ornaments; performance of rituals for pacification and appeasement or attainment of worldly prosperity, preparations of divine medicines or chemicals, interview with one's master, business and collection of food grains; entry into a newly constructed house, service, cultivation, seed sowing, auspicious works and efforts for peace.

The flow of Ida (left nostril) is also favourable to these : Beginning of study, meeting with relatives, in birth and emancipation, and in initiation in religion and sacrifice, knowledge of times (past, present and future), tying quadruped animals on arrival in the house, in the treatment of serious diseases and at the time of addressing one's master; riding a horse or mounting an elephant, taking a new bow, tying an elephant or a horse performance of benevolent acts and establishment of a treasure ; in singing, playing on a musical instrument, dancing, study of the science of dancing, entry into a village or town, wearing the sandle-paste mark on the forehead, and the purchase of land.

The Ida is favourable when one is thinking about a sick relative, or is brooding over his illness, fever, or state of senselessness, and at the time of storage of food-grains or fuel-wood.

The moon Nadi (Ida) is favourable at the time of puttings on dental ornaments by ladies, coming of rains, worship of the preceptor, removal or purge of poisonous materials.

Although Ida has been declared as favourable for Yogic practices, yet when he Vayu and Akasha Elements are predominant in the Ida then it should be avoided.

All works whether at day or at night are successful under the flow of Ida. In fact the flow of Moon (Ida) is favourable for all auspicious works.

Effects of the flow of Pingala :

A study or teaching of cruel and destructive sciences, company of a woman, prostitution and boarding a big ship, corrupt works, drinking, worship of some Vira-mantra (mantra for obtaining vigour and bravery), in a state of restiveness, in the destruction of the country and poisoning the enemies, practice fo Shastras, journey, hunting, selling cattle and rubbing or breaking of bricks, wood, stone or jewel.

The Sun Nadi (Pingala or right nostril), is also favourable for : Practice of going out , ascent on a Yantra, Tantra, fort or a mountain, gambling, theft, taming an elephant or a horse, driving a chariot, Satakarmas (six ritualistic practices) such as Marana, and Uchchatana (also one of the Saatkarmas meaning expulsion or

42

repulsion), or in obstructiong a Yakshini, Vetala, poison and evil spirits; riding an ass, camel, buffalo, elephant or horse, crossing a torential river, practice of medicine and writing a manuscript; in Maran, Mahana and Stambhana (practices known as Satakarmas), enemity, Uchchatana and Vasikarana (practices known as Satakarmas), pressing anyone to do something, cultivation, anger and giving or accepting charity ; invocation of a spirit, opposition, eradication of an enemy, punishment, holding a sword, war against an opponent, carnal pleasures, seeking a king, taking food, bathing and works of illumination.

Those who know say that taking food, activating the appetite and increasing digestive fire, captivating a woman and sleeping can all be done best under the Sun Nadi (pingala or right nostril).

All the cruel works and various types of works requiring movement are successful under the Sun Nadi. There should not be a second thought about it.

Effects of Susumna

When the wind flows at one moment in the left nosttril and the next moment in the right nostril, it should be known as Susumna Nadi and it makes everything infructuous.

The fire residing in the sun nadi burns like Kala(death) and one should know this fire a poison and all-destructive.

When transaggressing their orders both the Nadis (left and right nostrils flow in a person then it is inauspicious for him. There is no doubt about it.

When the wind flows for a moment in the left and next moment in the right, it should be called irregular; and O Parvati ! it gives adverse results.

Irregular flows of the Nadis is said by the Pandits to be like a poison. One should do neither cruel nor

45

auspicious works and if one does so they all become infructuous.

In living, dying, questioning, profit, loss, victory, defeat, and in the flow of adverse and irregular Swara (flow of Susumna) one should always remember the Supreme Lord.

On such an occasion concentrating his mind on the Iswara one should indulge in Yogic practices only. No effort towards victory, benefit or comfort should be made in this condition.

When the Susumna flows during the reign of Surya Nadi (Pingala) then both a curse or a boon become ineffective.

46

During the transitional period of Nadi and Elements no auspicious work should be done. Even one should abstain from righteous act like charity etc.

When the irregular Swara rises then one should not even think of a work. If one does so he will meet adverse effects or even suffering and death – there is no doubt about it.

When the left Swara is followed by the Moon Swara and thereafter the right Swara is followed by the Sun Swara, then one should know both these orders as blank.

47

If before and after the left Swara, a messenger comes and takes his place on the left side, or if before or after the right Swara a messenger comes and takes place on the right side, then it is auspicious in both the cases.

If during the flow of a beginningless irregualr Susumna, one, remaining without food and fully engrossed, ontains absorption in the Subtle Brahman, then such a Susumna is called Sandhya by the knowers.

The Pandits do not consider knowing as Veda, and in fact Vedas are not mere knowing. The erudites call that as Veda from which one can obtain the knowledge of the Supreme Spirit.

48

The knowers do not call Sandhya
as the junction. Nor can Sandhya be
called a junction (Sandhi); but when
the Prana resides in the iregualar
junction then it is called Sandhi.

Devi said :

O God of Gods ! O Mahadeva ! O
Redeemer of all the Worlds ! Kindly,
tell me that secret which resides in
your hearts.

Iswara said :

There is no Ista-devata (desired deity)
beyond the Mystery of the knowledge

49

of Swaras. A Yogi who knows this is in reality a perfect Yogi.

The Creation takes place out of Five Elements and it also dissolves in the Elements. The Five Elements are the supreme Elements, and the Brahaman alone is beyond the Elements.

The Yogis through the Siddhis of Yoga try to know the names of the Elements. A person who considers Swaras as the best knowledge can know the evil symptoms of all types of men.

One who knows this Five-Elemental Universe made up of Water,

Fire, Wind, Earth and Akash, is respected and worshipped everywhere.

The bodies of all the Jivas (livings things) residing in the Lokas (worlds) spreading from Earth to Satyaloka do not differ from the point of view of Elements, but there is Nadi-differentiation in each case.

Five risings each have been located in each of the left and right sides. O My Beauty ! I will now tell you the eight-fold science of Tattvas, which please listen.

First comes the counting of Elements ; second is the Sandhi (midpoint or junction) of the breathing ; third comes the signs of the Swaras;

51

fourth is the location or place of the Swaras; fifth is the colour of the Elements (tatvas); sixth the Prana; seventh the taste-difference; and the eight the symptoms of the movement. In this way there are eight types of Pranas in all the moving and stationary creation. O Devi ! There is no knowledge beyond the science of Swaras.

One should start the determination of the Swaras always from the morning onwards, because although the Yogis talk about the actions depending on loss or delay of time yet they have the capacity to recognize the Elements.

One should place both the left and right thumbs on the respective ears, both the middle fingers on both the nostrils, the Tarjanis on both the eyes, and the Anamikas and the little fingers of both hands on the mouth.

When one has done so (as directed above) then the knowledge of the Elements comes to him in the form of colours i.e. yellow colour for Earth, white for Water, red for fire, black for Vayu, and spotted color for Akash.

Placing a mirror one should throw his breath on it and try to see the form of the haze formed on it. Thus the Pandits (Scholars) should know the predominating Elements on the basis of the shape of the haze.

If the haze so formed is square, like half-moon, triangualr, or dotted then one should know it as the sign of the Akash Element.

If the breathed air is passing through the central part of the nostril it is indicative of Earth Element; if it is through the lower part it means Water Elements; if it is through the top most part it means Fire Elements; and if it is oblique through the sides it means Air Elements. If it is flowing in a rotating manner it indicates the Akash Element.

The color of water is white; of earth is yellow; of fire is red; or air is blue and of the akash is like the colour of clouds.

The fire elements resides on both the shoulders; the air element at the root of the navel; the earth element in the thighs; the water element in the lowest part of the feet; and the akash element in the forehead.

The taste of Earth is sweet; of Water is saline, of Fire bitter, of Air sour, and of Akash pungent.

The length of Swara of Air Element is eight Angulas (fingers); of Fire Element four fingers; of Earth Element twelve fingers; and that of Water Element sixteen fingers.

If the Swara flows in the upward direction it is indicative of death; if it flows in the downward direction it

55

indicates tranquility; if it flows in an oblique manner then one should do the acts of repulsing others (Uchchatana); and if it flows in the middle, one should do the obstructing acts (Stambhan). The effect of Akash element is moderate in all kinds of works.

When the earth element is dominant then one should do stationary works; when water element is dominant roving works can be done successfully; when the fire element is dominant cruel works are successful and when air element is dominant the acts like Uchchatana (repulsing others) and Marana (acts of killing others) are successful.

No work should be done when the Akash element is dominating

56

because everything draws a blank during its reign. However, Yoga Sadhana can be done during its dominance.

The Earth and Water Elements provide Siddhi (success), Fire Element provides death; the Air Element provides destruction or loss, and the Akash Element makes everything infructions – so should such persons know who possess the knowledge of the Tattavas.

The Earth Element gives considerable success; the Water Element gives immediate profit, the Air and Fire Elements provide loss, and the Akash Element makes things unsuccessful.

When there is yellow colour, the Swara is moving consistently and with a moderate speed with the heaviness of its sound experienced upto the chin, and which may be slightly warm then one should know it to be the dominance of the Earth Element which provides success in all kinds of stationary works.

That which flows downwards, whose sound is heavy, which is fast in speed, which may be slightly cold, and whose distance may be sixteen fingers, should be known as the Swara of Water dominance, and under it one should do only auspicious works.

One that moves in a circular form, which is slightly warm, whose color is red, whose distance is four fingers and which flows in an upward direction, is the Swara of Fire Element and one should do only cruel works under it.

One that is temperate, whose colour is dark, which flows in an oblique direction, and whose distance is eight fingers, should be known as the Swara of Air Elements and only roving business are successful under it.

The Swara which flows with the qualities of all other Elements should be known as that of Akash Element and it is the Swara which makes the objects of Yogis successful.

The Swara whose color is yellow, which is square in shape and sweet in

59

taste which flows through the middle and whose length is twelve fingers, is called Earth Element and it bestows all prosperity.

The Swara whose colour is white, which is like half-moon in shape, whose taste is sweet and astringent, which is wet, and the length of whose flow is sixteen fingers, is Water Element and it gives all benefits.

The Swara whose color is red and shape triangualar, whose taste is pungent, which flows upwards and whose length is four fingers, should be known as the Fire Elements.

The Swara which is blue in colour, sour in taste, which moves in

an oblique direction, which is never still
and the length of whose flow is eight
fingers, should be known as the Wind
Element.

That Swara which is colour,
taste, flow, and direction of movement
is an assortment of all other Swaras,
should be known as the Akash Element
and it makes every work infructuous.

The Earth and Water Elements
are auspicious; the Fire Element gives
a middling result, and the Akasha and
the Wind Elements give inauspicious
results, loss and death.

The Earth Element extends from
East to West; the Wind Element

61

resides in the North, and in the middle is situated the Akash Element.

When there is a predominance of Earth or Water Elements under the moon Swara, or there is Fire Element under the Sun Swara, then it bestows success to all good or bad works, there is no doubt about it.

Earth element is beneficial during the day time and the Water Element during the night time. There is death from Fire element, destruction from Wind element and from Akash element often there can be loss due to fire.

The Earth element is considered favourable for preservation of life, victory, profit, agriculture, efforts towards earning money, mantra sadhana, war, asking questions from anyone, going out or returning.

If there is a dominance of the Water element then one should expect the arrival of the enemy; when there is a dominance of the Earth element it is auspicious; when there is a predominance of the Wind element then the enemy may go else where.; and when there is a predominance of Fire or Akash elements then it will cause loss or death of the enemy.

If someone asks a question when the Earth element is dominant there will be anxiety about vegetation (trees etc.). When the question is asked during the predominance of the Water or Wind elements then there will be

63

anxiety for life; and when the Fire element is predominant then there will be anxiety for metal etc. When the Akash element is dominating there may be an absence of anxiety, i.e. there will be no anxiety at all.

If the Earth element is dominating then one will move in company of several persons; if the Water and Wind elements are dominating he will move alone; when the Fire element is dominating he will move along with another person (i.e. two persons would move together); and if the Akash element is dominating then one would not move at all.

When the right Swara is flowing then in the Fire element the Mars, in the Earth element the Sun, in the

Water element the Saturn and in the Wind element the Rahu dominates.

When the left swara is flowing then in the water element the moon, in the earth element the mercury , in the wind element the jupiter, and in the fire element the venus dominate. All these planets always dominate in all works under the respective Swaras and Elements.

Mercury resides in the earth, moon in the water, sun and mars in the fire, rahu and saturn in the wind and jupiter in the akash elements.

If rahu is residing in the sun swara (i.e. right nostril flowing) and someone happens to ask a question

65

about the whereabouts of a person who has gone to some other place then he should be answered that the person in question has already moved to some other place from the place he had originally gone to.

If the water element is dominating at the time of the question then the reply should be that the person who has gone out would soon return. If the earth element is dominating the answer should be that the person who has gone out is spending his time well at the place where has gone. If the wind element is dominating then the answer should be that the person in question has moved further to some other place. If the fire element is dominating then the answer should be that the person in question is already dead.

When the earth element is dominating then one should know about the vegetations (trees etc); when the water element is dominating then one should know it for auspicious works; when the fire element is dominating then one should know about the metals; and when the akash element is dominating then one should know it to be blank, i.e. one should not express his knowledge about anything.

At the time of a question about someone, who has gone out if there is either earth or water element then the person in question is enjoying a satisfied life, good health, love of others, sufficient entertainment, victory and pleasure. If there is fire or the wind element then the person in question is suffering from fever with shivering or excessive sleep.

If the akash element is there, then the person in question should be pronounced dead. These twelve questions have been said in respect of the dominance of th elements. The persons who know should note them carefully.

The earth, water, fire, and wind elements are powerful in the east, west, south, and north directions respectively.

O Parvati ! This body is Five-Elemental, i.e. it is made up of Earth, Water, Fire, Wind and Akash Elements. And there are five qualities of earth in

68

this body in the form of bones, flesh, skin, nadis, and fifth the hairs of the body. Thus say the persons who are the masters of the Vedas and Shastras, i.e. Brahmajnani.

The Brahmajnanis say that the Semen, blood, fat, urine, and the fifthe the saliva are the quallities of Water.

According to the Brahmajnanis hunger, thirst, sleep, letharginess, and lustre are the five qualities of fire.

And the Vedantas say that running, walking, tying a knot, contraction and expancion are the five qualities of wind.

The knowers of Vedanta further say that love, enemity, shyness, fear, and attachment are the five qualities of akash.

In this body the earth resides for fifty Palas, the water for forty Palas, fire for thirty Palas, wind for twenty Palas, and the akash for ten Palas, that is from earth onwards the period of each of the subsequent element decreases by ten Palas respectively.

If the earht is reigning then the benefit or profit would come after a long time, if the water is reigning the benefit or profit would come almost immediately, if the wind is reigning then the quantum of benefit would be comparatively less, and if the fire is reigning then even a completed or successful work would be reversed or spoiled.

There are five qualities of earth, four of water, three of fire, two of wind, and one of akash , this is the knowledge of the Tattvas(Elements).

Hissing, blowing, broken and lying useless this earth provides results in all the works according to its condition.

Dhanistha, Rohini, Jyestha, Anuradha, Sravana, Abhijit, and Uttarasadha are the seven lunar mansions of earth element.

71

Purvasadha, Alesa, Mula, Ardra, Revati, Uttarabhadrapada and Satabhisa are the seven lunar manisons of water element.

Bharani, Krttika, Puysa, Maghi, Parvaphalguni, Purvabhadrapada, and Swati are the seven lunar mansion of fire element.

Visakha, Uttaraphalguni, Hasta, Citra, Punarvasu, Asvini and Mrgasira are the seven lunar mansions of wind element.

If a messenger sits on the side whose Nadi is flowing (either left side or the right side according to the flow of the left or right Nadi) and asks either auspicious or inauspicious questions then all the questions become fulfilled. If he asks a question from a vacant direction then his questions would draw a blank.

Even if the surya or Chandra (sun or moon) elements are flowing with their full strength in the breathing they do not provide success, but if there is a conjunction of both then it is giver of all kinds of success.

Sri Ramachandra (the legendry hero of Ramayana) and Arjuna (the hero of the war of Mahabharat-a) got their victories when superior elements were dominating; and all the Kauravas (rivals of Pandavas in the war of Mahabharata) were defeated and killed because elements were against them.

73

Some pure souls obtain the knowledge of the elements due to their Karmas of previous births or the kindness of their Gurus (teachers or masters).

The Bija of earth is Lam which should be meditated upon as residing in a square, yellow, shining like gold, and full of sweet fragrance. One who does so obtains a shining and fine body.

The Vam Bija should be meditated in the water element. It is like a half moon in shape. One who meditates upon it is not troubled by the pains of hunger and thirst. He can also remain submerged in water, i.e. he does not experience any difficulty even if he is drowned in water.

74

Ram is the Bija of agani element which is triangular in shape and red in colour. It is worth meditating and one who does so gains tolerance of intense furry of sun and fire and can devour any amount of food.

Yam is the Bija of wind element. Its shape is round and colour black. It should be meditated upon and one who does so can fly in the air like birds.

Ham is the Bija of akash element and is formless and of extra brightness. One who meditates upon it gains a knowledge of past, present and future and also gets Anima etc. Siddhis.

There is no wealth better than the place where a person with th knowledge of swara resides. A person who moves with the knowledge of swaras gets success without any efforts.

Parvati said :

O God of Gods, Mahadeva ! O Shankara ! How does this great science of Swarodaya provide the knowledge of past, present and future?

Ishwara said :

O my Beauty ! The knowledge of obtaining wealth in all the three times (past, present, and future) also victory

76

in all the three times comes from Swarodaya. There is no other science which would enable anyone to know about these.

The auspicious and inauspicious works are under Tattavas ; victory or defeat also is under the Tattvas; draught and prosperity are also under the Tattvas. Thus the Tattvas are said to be the cause of the works of all the three times.

Parvati said :

O God of Gods, Mahadeva ! Kindly tell me that which is the best friend of men and that which gives them success in this sea-like world.

77

Iswara replied :

O Lady of Beautiful face ! The Prana is the best friend and companion. There is no other well-wisher like it.

Parvati said :

How does the wind reside in the Prana, and is the body Prana-like? And meditating upon the elements how can the Yogis know about the Prana?

Shiva said :

Residing in this city-like body, the Prana is its guardian. This Prana measures ten fingers in inhalation and twelve fingers in exhalation.

It measures twenty four fingers when one is walking; forty two fingers when one is running, and sixtyfive fingers when one is doing sexual intercourse.

And O Devi ! the natural length of Prana is twelve fingers. At the time of taking food or vomitting its length becomes eighteen fingers.

If a Yogi succeeds in reducing the length of Prana even by one finger he obtains desirelessness. If he can reduce to two fingers he gets perfect bliss; and if he succeeds in reducing it by three fingers he gets the art of poetry.

If a Yogi reduces the length of Prana by four fingers he obtains Siddhi over speech; if he reduces by five fingers he gets the power of vision of far off things; if he can reduce to six fingers he can fly in the air; and if he reduces it by seven fingers he obtains tremendous speed.

If one succeeds in reducing the length of Prana to eight fingers he can get Anima etc., Siddhis; if nine fingers then he gets all the nine kinds of prosperity; if ten fingers he gets the power of assuming various shapes; and if he reduces it by eleven fingers the shadow of his body vanishes.

If the length of Prana is reduced by twelve fingers one gets the speed of a Hamsa and he drinks the nectar like waters of the river Ganges. If a Yogi fills the Prana from the tip of toe nails to Sikha (top of the head) then he needs no food for sustain his life, that is he conquers hunger and thirst.

Thus has been described the method of obtaining all kinds of successes through the control of Prana. This Knowledge comes only through the instructions of a Guru (teacher) and no amount of study and books can provide it.

If any chance one does not get the Moon Swara in the morning and the Sun Swara in the evening then it would come definitely by midnight.

If one has to go to fight in a distant place then the Moon Swara alone gives victory, and if the person puts that foot forward whose side of Swara is flowing while he is about to set out then he gets every success.

At the time of beginning a journey or in marriage, or while entering a house or a city the Moon Swara is always auspicious.

If on an equinoctial or solstitial point, tithi (date), or weekday, the Swaras and Elements flow with their ruling lords in a person then that person can win his enemy by a mere stoppage of his breath. Such a person does not get pain or difficulty in another world as well.

During a war if a person, putting on his armour repeats the syllables 'Jivam Raksha' (life protection), he survives and also gains victory over the entire world.

In pacificatory rituals one should proceed when the Earth or the Water is ruling; for adventurous or cruel rituals he should proceed under the Fire or the Wind element, and should do neither of these of rituals when the Akasha element is ruling.

One should consecrate the weapons with the Swara, i.e. should hold the weapon in the hand whose side of Swara is flowing. Similarly he should open the weapons and throw them (operate them) likewise. Thus doing he would always gain victory.

One who draws in the Prana-Vayu at the time of mounting a horse or other vehicle always gets success in his works.

If the materials of the enemy have a feeble strength of the swara and one's own materials have a strong Swara then such a person obtains victory all alone over the world.

If the Nadi which is flowing and the Deity and direction of the same Nadi are ruling then that gives success in all types of works.

84

First of all a person should perform a mudra then enter in a battle. One who performs Serpent Mudra (Sarpa mudra) gets his desires fulfilled, there is no doubt about it.

If at the time of the flow of Moon or Sun Swara the wind element is reigning and it becomes known to the knowers of the science of Swaras then good warriors come forward as allies. If the akash or the wind elements are flowing under the circumstances then there would be all destruction.

The army should be sent to fight in that direction in which the wind element is flowing. If it is done so then one would obtain victory even if Indra himself is the enemy – there is no doubt about it.

85

If one draws the string of the bow up to the ear of the side of that Nadi in which the wind element is flowing then he can win even Indra.

Even a very strong enemy can not destroy the strength of a warrior who defends all the parts of his body.

One who produces a sound from the joints of thumb and first finger and also from the toe, can gain victory over even a million warriors.

If a person goes out when the wind element is flowing either in the moon or the sun swara then he can protect the various directions and always gain victory.

86

If a messenger say something
which isdesired, from his mouth when
one is inhaling then that person on
going out gets all his desires fulfilled.

All the said or desired works are
fulfilled when one is inhaling and
destroyed when one is exhaling.

The right Nadi of men and left
Nadi of women is auspicious and at the
time of war the Kumbhaka Nadi is
superior. Thus there are only three
Nadis and their movements also only
three.

How can there be the knowledge
of swaras without knowing the
difference of Ha-kara and Sa-kara?

87

Therefore one always gains success through two words the 'Soham' and 'Hamsa'.

One get success by protecting the living organisms through filling the blank swara because the living organisms can meet destruction and the blank always protects the organisms.

If a questioner is putting a question regarding war while sitting either on the left or right, and if the swara is in full strength there will be no destruction. If the swara is blank then there can be death or destruction.

If at the time of a question the earth element is in the stomach, the water element in the feet, the fire element in the thighs, and the wind element in the hands then the person may be attacked by some weapons.

If the akash element is flowing then there may be a possibility of injury in the head. Thus five kinds of injuries have been described in this Science of Swaras.

If the moon swara is flowing at the time of a war then the opponent would definitely with and if the sun swara is flowing then the invader would gain victory.

If there is some doubt about victory during the war then one should see in the middle of the Nadi and if the

Prana-Vayu is flowing through the Susumna then the enemy would be in trouble in the war.

In a war one should stand in that direction whose Nadi is flowing i.e. if the moon nadi (Ida) is flowing then he should stand either in the east or north; if the sun nadi (pingala) is flowing then in the west or south of the enemy. One who fight in this manner will gain victory, there is no need to give a second thought to it.

If at the time of war the left Nadi is flowing then the enemy would win and may make the invader his captive.

If at the time of war the sun nadi is flowing continuously then the invader would gain victory even if he is fighting against the Devas (Gods) or Asuras (Demons).

One who enters in war under the flow of the left Nadi is abducted by the enemy. One who enters in war under the flow of the Susumna nadi would not meet any opposition. If one proceeds for war under the sun swara then he would gain victory.

In case two questioners ask two questions regarding war and if the full swara is flowing then the first questioner would win and if a blank swara is flowing then the second would win.

If one proceeds for a war under the full flow of a nadi then his enemy would come at his back i.e. the enemy would retreat after seeing his back. If he proceeds under the flow of a blank nadi then the enemy would come face to face and meet his death, there is no doubt about it.

When sitting on the left side one asks a question then if letters of the question or the letters of the subjects of the asked question are even in number then he would gain success or victory and if the number of letters is odd then he will be unsuccessful or defeated. If the questioner sits on the right side and asks a question then the results would be reversed, i.e. the even would be victorious and the odd would be defeated.

If at the time of question, the moon swara is flowing then there would be treaty among the fighting groups, and if it is the sun swara then the war would be there.

If the war begins under the earth element then the results would be equal for both the parties; if a war begins under the water element then the person who starts would win; if it begins under the fire element then the one who started it would meet his destruction, and if it begins under the akash element then he would die in the war.

If at the time of a question, due to some reason or mere complancency, one is not able to get a knowledge of the Swaras then a sensible person should act as follows :

He should drop a flower on the ground with a clear heart. If the flower falls on the ground by its face the results would be success and if it falls a little distance away on its sides then the result would be failure for the questioner.

If a person while either standing or sitting exhales its Prana-Vayu with a clear heart then all his works would be successful.

Death, various deadly weapons, serpents, disease, enemy or robbers can't damage a person whose Prana-Vayu is at the time in a vacant place.

The person should make the Vayu (air) still within his organisms, then start it also from within his organisms, and enter into gambling in the same state – he will definitely win.

All kind of powers become unsuccessful before the power of a person who is versed in the science of Swara because the knower of swara always remain powerful in this and also the next world.

Some possess the strength of ten, some of hundred , some of ten thousand, some of one lac (100000), and some of their kingdom, but the Gods like Indra and Brahma have millions of times more strength than them. Similarly, the knower of swaras

95

also has millions of times more strength than them.

Devi said :

You told me about the mode of victories by men in war, but if one has to fight against Yamaraja (the God of Death) then how should he gain victory?

Iswara (Mahadeva) said :

One who meditates upon the Gods with a still and undisturbed mind and submits the oblation of his organisms in Kumbhaka (i.e. stops his Prana-vayu (breathing)) gets his desires fulfilled, gains immense benefit and victory.

96

The world of form originated
from the Formless God. This world
manifests in form the moment one has
the knowledge of the Formless
Supreme Lord.

Devi said :

O Maheshwara ! You described the way
for victory in the fight with Yamaraja,
now kindly tell me the way of
captivating (vasikarana (hypnotism))
the Gods.

Ishwara said :

If one with his sun swara attracts the
moon swara of a woman and

97

establishes it within his Jiva-mandala then that woman would be captivated for ever, so have said the man who practice austerities. But succeeds only in case of one's own married wife.

The man should adopt the Jiva-swara of a woman with his own Jiva-swara, and extend his Jiva-swara to the Jiva-swara of the woman. When the Jiva-swara of the man resides thus in the Jiva-swara of the woman the man remains captivated by the woman throughout of his life.

The man who drinks the Susumna swara in the midnight when the woman is sleeping, keeps the Prana of the woman captivated.

After that time is a little past then if the man with the recitation of the Astakshara Mantra lends his moon swara to the woman then she instantly develops love for him.

When one is lying, when he is in intercourse with a woman, or just touching her, drinks the moon swara of the woman with his sun swara then his charm becomes captivating like the God of Love (Kamadeva).

If there is a conjunction of the Shiva swara (i.e. sun swara) and the Shakti swara (i.e. the moon swara) at the time of intercourse with a woman , or if the man gives his moon swara to the woman then that man can win over a hundred woman.

After lending his sun swara to the moon swara of a woman if there is companionship for 9, 7, 3 or 5 times, or putting his sun swara into the moon swara of the woman he meets the woman on 2, 4, or 6 times then that woman would be captivated.

Drawing his own sun swara and moon swara with the speed of a serpent one should put his lips on the lips of the woman and make the moon and sun swaras to meet as described above.

As long as the woman is under sleep so long the man should drink the nectar of the lips of the woman and when she wakes up he should kiss her neck and eyes.

100

A man should so captivate the woman. But it is my order that the method of captivation should not be divulged to a licentious or person of loose character.

ON FERTILISATION

On the fifth day from the day a woman is free from the monthly menstrual cycle and the sun swara of the man and the moon swara of the woman is flowing then an intercourse with the woman under such circumstances would give birth to a male child.

101

When the water and the earth elements are flowing then the woman should take cow milk mixed with Shankhavalli and request her husband three times for intercourse.

When the woman has taken the aforesaid medicine after the menstrual cycle then the man should enter into entercourse with her. This will produce a beautiful male child as brave as the lion among animals.

A person who enters into a intercourse during the flow of sun swara under the susumana swara then he will produce a deformed and ugly child.

102

After the menstruation on the odd days when the sun swara of the man flows during day and night and the moon swara of the woman, and the fertilisation takes place when either earth, water or fire elements are reigning then it will produce a child even to a sterile woman.

If at the beginning of the menstruation the sun swara of the man and the moon swara of the woman flows and both happen to cohabit then even a sterlite woman would also conceive.

If at the start of the intercourse the sun swara flows in the man and after the ejaculation the moon swara starts flowing then the woman would not conceive.

103

If at the time of a question from a preganant woman the moon nadi is flowing then she carries a daughter in her womb, if the sun swara flows then it is a son, and if both the swaras are flowing then there would be a premature abortion.

If at the time of a question, there si earth element then a daughter, if water then a son, if wind then also a daughter, if fire then an abortion, and if there is akash then an impotent would be born.

If at the time of question regarding the nature of the pregnancy the moon swara is there then a daughter, if sun swara then a son. If susumna then an impotent and if the body and limbs of the questioner are not suffering from any deformity then a son would be born.

O my Beauty ! If the questioner comes to the side of a vacant swara then there will be no birth at all, if both the swaras are running then there would be a birth of twins, and if there is an alteration of swaras, that is the susumna is flowing then there would be abortion – so should the knowers of Tattvas drive.

If the conception takes place under the wind element then the offspring would be giver of pain; if it takes place under the water element then an offspring famous in all directions and giver of comforts would be born; if it takes place under the fire element then either there will be abortion or the born baby would be short-lived; and if it takes place under the earth element then the offspring would be beautiful, wealthy and prosperous in life.

If the conception takes place under the water element the son born would spend a comfortable and enjoyabel life and his wealth would be never leave him. If the conception takes place under the akash element then there would be abortion.

If the conception takes place under the earth element then a son and if under the water element then a daughter would be born; and if takes place under the ramaining elements then there would either be an abortion or the child would die soon after birth.

One should obtain from his Guru at the earliest the knowledge as to how to know the existence of the moon swara in the middle of the sun and the sun swara in the middle of the moon. This can not, otherwise, be known through the study of Vedas or million of shastras (books).

ON PREDICTION OF WHOLE YEAR

On the first day of the lilghted fortnight of Chaitra (the first month of Hindu Calender) the erudite Yogis (saints) should try to see the summer and the winter solstces, and the differentiation of the swaras i.e. he should predict the

107

results for the whole year through the flow of the swaras.

If at the time of the rise of the moon swara there is either earth, water or the wind elements then there would be a good harvest.

If under the moon swara there is fire or the akash element then there would be serious famine and difficulty. Similarly one should know the results for the year and month of day according to the aforesaid order of the Tattvas.

The susumna nadi is considered cruel and bad for all types of works, and it causes the destruction of the country, epidemics, pains, difficulties and other calamities.

If one meditates over the differences of the swaras at the time of transition of the sun to the sign of Aries then the knower of Tattvas can predict results for the whole year.

If at the above time there are earth etc., elements then the predictions for the year, month and day would be auspicious and if there are akash, wind or fire elements then the results would be inauspicious.

If at the above time the earth element is reigning during the day then there will be prosperity, rich crop , sufficient rainfall and prosperous time.

109

If on the above day the water element is flowing then there will be sufficient rainfall, prosperity, freedom from diseases, and rich in the fields.

If the fire element is flowing then there would be famine, division of the country, scanty rainfall, and destruction of the productions.

If at the above time there is wind element then there would be trouble, calamity, fear, scanty rainfall, and excess of insects (such as mosquitoes etc.).

If at the above time, there is akash element then one should know the scantiness of crop and comfort.

110

If the swara enters in its fullness then the favourable elements would provide sufficient crops. If at the time of the rise of the elements the sun or the moon swaras are reversed, i.e. there is sun swara in place of the moon or vice versa, then it gives sufficient crops and prosperity.

If there is fire or akash element in the right swara and if one starts hoarding then there may be deerness all around within two months.

If in the night sun nadi is flowing and in the morning the moon nadi starts flowing and there is a conjunction of the akash, wind and fire elements then there would be numerous calamities on the earth.

111

ON THE PREDICTION OF DISEASES

If at the time of the question there is earth element then diseases due to one's own fate, if there is water element then diseases due to excessive hydration, and if there is fire element then diseases caused by aberrations in the phlegm, or pain, would occur.

If the questioner comes first towards the vacant side of the swara and then shifts to the swara which is flowing then the patient, even if he is in a state of coma, would definitely survive.

If a questioner (regarding the welfare of someone who is ill) sits on the side whose swara is flowing and asks a question then the patient would definitely survive the illness.

If the right nadi is flowing and the questioner happens to utter something very bad, the patient would yet live. If the moon (left) nadi is flowing then the result would be status quo.

One should considered his own swara. Now if the questioner taking his place on that side whose swara is flowing, asks a question regarding the life (of the patient) he will get the fruit of the patient's life.

113

If a questioner asks a question at the inhalation of either the left or right nadi, then his desire would be fulfilled – there is no doubt about that.

If at the time of a question the questioner takes his place at a lower place then his patient would definitely survive, but if he takes a higher place his patient would meet his death.

If there is a rise of susumna and the questioner happens to ask his question from a blank nadi with the number of letters of his question being odd (1, 3, 5, etc.) then the result would be against him.

If one's own swara is in the place of the moon, and the questioner takes

114

his place on the sun side then his patient, even if treated by a hundred phusicians would yet meet his death.

If one's own swara is flowing through Pingala and the quenstioner taking his seat on the left side asks a question, then still his patient would die if Maheshawara(lord Shiva) himself is protecting him.

If even one element is adverse the disease becomes acute; if two elements are adverse then there is a danger from the friends and relatives; and if this state continues for two fortnights (i.e. one month) there is certain death.

PREDICTIONS REGARDING AGE AND DEATH

On the basis of the movement of Vayu (air) an ble person should examine the time of death in the order of month, fortnight and year.

The life of that person becomes stabilised who moistens his five-elemental body with the oil fo Shiva's love and preserves it with the sun-like wind.

A person who, controlling the flow of air in his breaths avoids the sun swara throughout the day time, can thus enjoy a long life through this practice of arresting the sun.

116

Because the moon roams in the sky its beams falling down moisten the body like lotus. Thus, if a Karma-Yogi takes the shelter of moon through practice, he becomes immortal.

One who keeps practicing to avoid the moon swara in the night and the sun swara in the day, is the real Yogi – there is no doubt about it.

If the breath of a person flows throughout the night through one nostril then he would within three years, meet his death.

According to the knowers of elements if the breath of a person remains flowing through Pingala for two consecutive nights then he has a life of only two years.

A person whose breath ramains flowing through one nostril for three consecutive nights has, according to those who know, one year of life.

A person in whom there is a consistent flow of moon swara in the night and the sun swara in the day will meet his death within six months.

A person who on looking at the reflection of the sun in water finds the sun's disc cut in the south, west, north or east directions, has a life span of six, three, two or one month respectively, viz., if he sees the disc cut in the southern direction he has a life-span of three months, if in the north a life-span of two months, and if in the east a lilfe-span of only one month. If the reflection has a hole in the centre then only ten days of life are left and if the entire reflection appears to be rotating then he will meet his death that very day. The omniscient sages heve so said about the apparent span of one's life.

If a question regarding the welfare of a patient is put forth by the messengers of the following descriptions then the patient would die : if the messenger is putting on a black loin cloth; has injuries in his teeth; has his head shaved; is holding a rope in his hand with a body rubbed with oil; is poor; is in tears while asking the question; has ashes, burning embers, skull or a pestle in his hand; comes after sunset, and whose legs are benumbed.

Sudden mental disturbances, sudden aberration in the senses, and sudden development of good qualities are all symptoms of delirium.

Listen now my own observations about one whose body is cold, whose mind is disturbed, and whose body develops unfavourable symptoms (specially of approaching death.).

One who utters words portentious of inauspicious meaning, who speaks incorrect words and later repents over it, will soon die, there is no doubt about it.

120

Whose Humkara (roar) is cold and whose hissing is like fire, definitely dies even though protected by physicians.

A patient who is not able to see clearly any of these, viz., his toungue, the sky, pole star, feet of Vishnu, the Matrikas, Arundhati, Moon, Venus or Agasti, would definitely die within a year.

One who can't see the sun, moon or fire and also their rays, has only eleven months of life left for him.

One who either in the waking state or in a dream, sees a pool full of human excreta, urine, gold or silver, will not live beyond ten months.

A person who does not see a lamp or gold rubbed on a touchstone, or sees deformity in all the species would not live beyond nine months.

If a man's nature changes suddenly, i.e. if he is fat but suddenly becomes lean and thin or vice versa, or his black complexion suddenly changes to glistening golden colour, or being brave and courageous he suddenly becomes meek and coward, or being religious becomes altogether irreligious, or still, being of a composed temperament becomes of an unstable temperament, then he would live only for eight months.

122

A person who develops pain in the palm of his hand or at the root of his tongue, or whose blood becomes blackish and he does not feel pain even if pinched, would die within seven months.

A person whose medial fingers (first, middle and third fingers of the land) do not bend, whose throat becomes dry even without any disease, who inspite of repeated questions is unable to give consistent replies, would die within six months.

A person whose breast-skin becomes insensitive, will definitely be borne on the shoulders of four persons (i.e. die) within five months.

123

A person whose eyes lose their sight but suffer from pain, would die within four months.

A person whose teeth and testicles do not experience pain when pressed, would die within three months.

I now declare briefle that science of Shiva with which one can foresee the Kala (death) although it may still be far away.

One should go to a desolate place and then placing the sun on his back try to see carefully the neck of his shadow. Thereafter, if looking at the

124

sky, he recites the Mantra 'Hrim Parabrahmane Namah' one hundred and eight times he will see the lord Shankara whose appearance is like pure crystal and who can assume numerous forms. One who practices it for six months becomes a king and if he continues to practice for two years he can become the creator, the destroyer and the lord of his self. If he cotinues the practice ever after he will obtain the knowledge of all the three times, the past, present, and future, get perfect bliss and nothing will remain inaccessible to him.

A Yogi who sees (in the aforesaid manner) the complexion of Shiva as black would meet his death within six months, there is no doubt about it.

125

If he sees the complexion (of Shiva) as yellow he will suffer from fear; if blue then he will suffer loss; and if he sees it multihued then that Yogi would achieve Siddhis (supernatural powers).

If he can not, in the reflection, see the feet, ankles, belly or hands then the Yogi would definitely meet his death.

If he is unable to see the left hand then his wife would meet certain death; if unable to see the right hand his kinsmen would meet destruction, and in a month's time he would himself die.

126

Death would come to him within a month who is unable to see the head; within eight days if unable to see the thighs or shoulders; and immediately if unable to see the shadow at all.

Putting one's back to the sun in the morning if the fingers and lips of the shadow are not visible then one would meet his death within a second; if the entire shadow and his own person is not visible then he would die within half a second. Same would be the fate if the ears, shoulders, hands, mouth, sides, and heart are not visible. If the head of the shadow in not visible and the person also loses the knowledge of the directions (east etc.) then he would survive only for six months.

127

If the sun swara flows continuously in a person for sixteen days, then that person would die within fifteen days.

If in a person only the sun swara flows continuously and the moon swara does not flow at all, then he would die within a fortnight.

If in a person, the excreta, urine and wind come out simultaneously then he should know that it is time for death and he would end his life within ten days.

If in a person the moon swara continues to flow and the sun swara does not flow even once, then he

128

would die within a month – so say the persons having knowledge of death.

If one is unable to see the Pole-star, Arundhati, three feet of Vishnu, and fourth the Matrikas (all names of stars or constellations) then he should know that no life is left for him. Here the tongue is called Aundhati, tip of the nose Pole Star, eyebrows the feet of Vishnu and the Stars as Matrikas.

Death would certainly come to him within nene days who is unable to see the eyebrows within seven days who is uable to hear any sound by his ears, within three days who is unable to see the stars, and within a day who is unable to see his tongue.

129

One should lightly press the inner corners of the eyes and if by doing so he does not see a light-spot then he should know that he will die within ten days.

One can avert death by bathing in the Tirthas (sacred places) , charity, austerity, righteous actions, recitation of mantras, concentration and Yoga.

Impurities and humours destroy the body but the equilibrium of wind imcreases the vigour and strength.

One should perfect his body by religious practices. Practice of Yoga provides success; Yoga makes the impossible possible, and in the absence of Yogic practices one meets his death

130

because there is no other way of averting it.

A person whose heart illumines with the beginningless and unique knowledge of the Shiva Swarodaya that destroyes all darkness and whose brilliance is pleasant like the moon, has no fear of death even in his dreams.

The Ida is Ganges, Pingala is Yamuna, and the central (susumna) is the Saraswati. The confluence of these three should be know as the Prayaga.

First is Sadhana. Therefore, one should sit in Padmasana and then practice Uddiyana, i.e. train the movement of Apana-Vayu upwards to bring it to the navel.

131

In order to purify their bodies in all respects the Yogis should obtain the knowledge of Pranayama in its three aspects of Puraka, Kumbhaka, and Rechaka.

Of these the Puraka (drawing in of the external air) nourishes the body development and brings equilibrium in all the humours, while the Kumbhaka (stopping the movement of internal and external air) protects the organisms by keeping the body humours at their places.

The Rechaka (exhalation of the internal air) destroys evil deeds. Thus one who practices Pranayama obtains the place of Yoga. A Yogi who is able to stabilize his breathing can stop death.

According to his capacity one should stop in a natural way the air through Kumbhaka. Then an able person should practice Rechaka by the moon swara and Puraka by the sun swara.

Whose sun swara drinks the moon swara from time to time and vice versa, will live till the moon and the stars exist.

A Yogi who stops nadi which is flowing and also closing his mouth does not allow the air so stopped to escape through the mouth becomes young again even his old age.

133

One should stop with his fingers his mouth, nose, eyes and ears (i.e. assume the Yoni Mudra) and know it as the rise of Tattavas and the pleasant Sanmukhikarana (making six mouths). This implies that a Yogi can thus know in the world the form, movement, taste, region and symptoms of the elements and also their individual paths in their interactional process.

Desireless and pure Yogi should not worry about anything. By renunciation of desires he can effortlessly obtain victory over death.

The entire world is known through the power of eyes. Therefore, if the mind of a Yogi concentrates for a

134

Prahara (about three hours) on that power, then the age of that Yogi increases at the rate of three Ghatikas everyday – so has Shiva said in the Tantrashastras for the benefit of the qualified Siddhas.

A Yogi, sitting in Padmasana, should stop the Apana-vayu situated in the Anal region, raise it upwards and then merge it with the Prana-vayu. When both have merged and reached in the susumna then they should be taken through the Brahmarandhra and released in the path of sky. Thus, devoted to the feet of Shiva, the Yogis who leave (i.e. die) enjoy eternal Bliss.

The Yogi who knows it and always studies it becomes rid of all pains and gets all the desired fruits.

135

A person who has the knowledge of swaras, always has Lakshmi (wealth) at his feet and obtains all pleasures and comforts wherever he goes.

Just as in all the Vedas the Pranava, or of all the Brahmanas sun is worth worshipping so in this world the knowers of swara are to be worshipped.

Even millions of medicinal mixtures can't equal a person who knows all the aforesaid three Nadis, and also has the knowledge of the Tattvas.

There is nothing on earth to
repay the debt of even one word given
by a person who knows the Nadi-bheda
(knowledge of differentiation of the
Nadis).

The results of war, captivation of
women, pregnancy and diseases all
can be predicted to the precision of
half a Kala (measure of time) through
the knowledge of Swaras and their
elements.

Thus, came the science of
Swarodaya to this world and was
propagated by Yogis. One who recites
it during the lunar or solar eclipses,
obtains all Siddhis (supernatural
powers).

137

One who keeps sitting at his place, takes little food, practices concentration and knows the Supreme Lord will obtain the knowledge of Swaras.

THE ENDS OF THE SCIENCE OF SWARODAYA REVEALED IN THE CONVERSATION OF SHIVA AND PARVATI.

Made in United States
Orlando, FL
28 August 2023

36506322R10078